For Edward

Composer's World

Pyotr Ilyich Tchaikovsky

VIKING

INTRODUCTION

A Russian troika

Asked to name their favorite classical composer, many people would answer, "Tchaikovsky." His music has always had a special appeal: memorable tunes, whether passionately eloquent or stylishly graceful; wild, abandoned dance-music; the sheer exuberance of pieces such as the *1812 Overture* or the famous opening of the First Piano Concerto; and masterly handling of a vast palette of orchestral color — these are qualities that go straight to the hearts of his listeners. Where Brahms' music is often demanding, Tchaikovsky's is always easy to listen to — it seems to give nothing but pleasure, even at its most tragic and overwhelmingly emotional. Yet Tchaikovsky was himself a moody, melancholy man, whose private life was often deeply unhappy. This was partly the result of his own temperament: he was a hypochondriac, and also a homosexual at a time when this was regarded as a secret shame and disgrace. But he was also Russian, and inclined, like many of his countrymen, to displays of extreme emotion.

Tchaikovsky's Russia was a vast, inhospitable land, bordering on the Baltic Sea, Prussia, and Austria–Hungary in the west, and the Sea of Japan in the east. Its northern territory included the icy wastes of Siberia, inhabited only by wolf packs and exiled political prisoners, and much of it lay inside the Arctic Circle; while to the south, it stretched as far as the arid Mongolian steppes, the mountains of Turkestan and the Caucasus, and the Mediterranean climates of the Black and Caspian Seas. Nearly all the major towns and cities lay in the west, between the Austro-Hungarian border and the Ural mountains, and communications were primitive; it was not until the mid-nineteenth century that a railway line was built between Russia's two principal cities, Moscow and St. Petersburg. For peasants the main means of transport was an ox-cart; while the aristocracy and middle classes used either horse-drawn carriages in the summer, or, in the winter, sleighs — the famous three-horse *troikas*, with their brightly colored harnesses and bells jingling over the deep snow.

This huge empire was ruled by one person — the Tsar, commonly believed to have been appointed by God (like the Kings of England until the seventeenth century). The Tsar made all the political decisions; there was no parliament, and the views of ordinary people were not represented. In order to keep people in order, tsars employed brutal methods, using spies and secret police to inform on any dissident activity, and the army to crush any revolts. Most Russians were very poor: until 1861 the peasants, or serfs, lived under a feudal system, which meant that they were owned by their masters, and had no rights at all. Such systems of government had long been abandoned in the rest of Europe, but Russian society was still run on medieval lines, with all its barbarity and injustice. Not surprisingly, the intelligent, educated middle classes – the artists, writers, and students – often rebelled against the repressive system, and there were many attempts to assassinate the tsars and establish a more acceptable régime. Even Alexander II, one of the most liberal tsars, who in 1861 freed all the serfs and introduced cautious reforms, was blown up in his carriage by a terrorist's bomb. His grandson was Nicholas II, whose political incompetence led to the 1917 Revolution. He too was murdered, along with all his family, at the end of the First World War – an act of violence which brought the last great European dynasty with absolute power to an abrupt end.

But while life was miserable for the majority of Russians, with starvation and disease always waiting to pounce, the educated middle classes were no worse off than other Europeans of their time. Since political activity was a dangerous game, likely to lead to death or exile, they turned instead to their national roots, finding a rich vein of folk-culture – including bloody stories of Russia's savage past, or charming fairy tales – to explore in art, literature, and music. Although many of Russia's greatest writers found their works subject to rigid and narrow-minded censorship, they sowed the seeds of a great nineteenth-century flowering of the arts. In the eighteenth century, there was no native Russian classical music: it had all been imported from Italy and France; and just as Alexander Pushkin (1799–1837) is regarded as the father of Russian literature, so the foundation of a national Russian musical style was laid by Mikhail Glinka (1804–1857) with his two operas, *A Life for the Tsar* and *Ruslan and Lyudmila*. Glinka paved the way for a group of "nationalist" composers, who used folk subjects and folk themes in their music; but by fusing this rich heritage with the Western symphonic tradition, it was Tchaikovsky who ultimately achieved a place amongst the first rank of European composers.

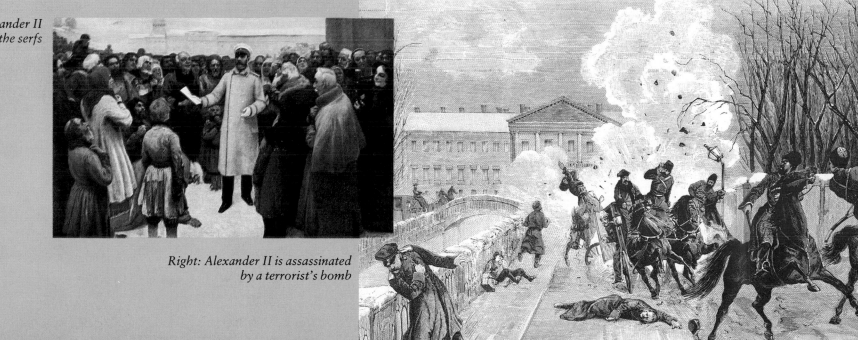

Alexander II freeing the serfs

Right: Alexander II is assassinated by a terrorist's bomb

1 Childhood

Pyotr Ilyich Tchaikovsky was born on May 7, 1840, in Kamsko-Votkinsk, a medium-sized industrial town in the Vyatka province, about 600 miles east of Moscow. His father, Ilya Petrovich, was a down-to-earth mining engineer and Chief Inspector of the metal works: it was from his nervous, epileptic mother that Pyotr Ilyich – their second son – inherited his tendency to real or imagined ill-health, fits of hysteria, and deep depression.

Ilya Petrovich Tchaikovsky was a person of some standing in Votkinsk, able to provide a spacious and comfortable home for his wife and four children. When he was still a tiny child, Pyotr listened eagerly to tunes from fashionable Italian operas played on the family's orchestrion, a kind of mechanical barrel-organ which could roughly reproduce musical sounds. In September 1844, Tchaikovsky's mother Alexandra visited St. Petersburg and her husband reported proudly that "Sasha [Pyotr's sister, who was not yet two] and Pyotr have written a song, 'Our Mama in Petersburg.'"

Alexandra Tchaikovsky brought back a young French governess, called Fanny Dürbach, for her eldest son Nikolay. Soon Pyotr was asking to join the lessons, and by the time he was six he was reading both French and German. Fanny became very fond of the whole family, and especially of Pyotr, whom she found so hypersensitive that she called him a "porcelain child" – the slightest scolding would reduce him to floods of tears. She was also worried by his addiction to music, which often seemed to upset him: one night after a party she found him awake, pointing to his forehead, and crying, "Oh this music, this music! Take it away! It's in here and it won't let me sleep!"

The house where Tchaikovsky was born

Fanny Dürbach, Tchaikovsky's governess

Alexandra Andreevna, the composer's mother

Three months before Pyotr's eighth birthday his father resigned his post, and shortly afterwards the family moved to St. Petersburg, Peter the Great's elegant city, built on graceful, classical architectural lines by the shores of the Baltic Sea. St. Petersburg was Russia's "window on the West," and it was the major cultural center of nineteenth-century Russia – the place where the Tsar and the aristocracy had their palaces, and middle-class intellectuals their homes. Pyotr was sent to a fashionable boarding school. Separation from his family made him thoroughly miserable, until an attack of measles, from which he failed to recover quickly, kept him out of school for six months. Then his father found a new job in Alapayevsk, on the other side of the Ural mountains, and the family moved again. But after the arrival of twin brothers called Anatoly and Modest, "the most terrible event" of his whole childhood happened: his mother, busy with her new babies, decided to enroll him in the junior department of the School of Jurisprudence in St. Petersburg, where boys were trained to enter the civil service. When the day came for Pyotr to enter the school, he was so hysterical at the thought of parting from his mother that he tried to throw himself under the wheels of her carriage as she drove away. From that day on, he was terrified of being abandoned.

Pyotr was no more happy at his new school, which was run like a military academy, than his old one. But in the

The river Neva at St. Petersburg

1840-1854

Ilya Petrovich Tchaikovsky, the composer's father, with his twin sons Modest and Anatoly

month of his twelfth birthday his family returned to St. Petersburg, and his new-found security and happiness encouraged him to pass his entrance exams to the School of Jurisprudence itself, and also to make some real friends among his schoolfellows. But just two years later, his life was once more overturned by a devastating tragedy. As part of the Asian continent, Russia had always been open to the spread of cholera epidemics, and from 1853 to 1854 the hideous disease once more raged unchecked. In June 1854, Tchaikovsky's mother fell ill. The doctors did everything they could, but one of the few remedies they knew was to immerse the patient, whose skin felt icy cold, in a scalding hot bath. The shock of this treatment proved too much for Alexandra: she died almost instantly in great agony. Pyotr, who had always been exceptionally close to his mother, was shattered: he always remembered vividly the horror of her death, and he could not speak or write about it for two years.

St. Petersburg today

С. Петербургъ — St.-Pétersbourg   Консерваторія — Le Conservatoire

2 Adolescence

After his mother's sudden death, Pyotr grew much closer to his younger sister Alexandra, a gentle, affectionate girl who in turn was to support him throughout his own crises. He also tried to comfort himself with music, making one or two attempts at composition, and in the autumn of 1854 he began to take singing and piano lessons. His progress was unspectacular – one of his teachers later recalled that "certainly he was gifted, he had a good ear and a good memory, a fine touch, but otherwise there was nothing, absolutely nothing, that suggested a composer, or even an excellent performer." Even his first printed composition – an Italian-style song called *Mezza Notte* (Midnight) – showed little hint of great talent. Meanwhile, under the influence of an eccentric Neapolitan singing teacher called Luigi Piccioli – a man who dyed his hair, used make-up and smoothed out his wrinkles with a "do-it-yourself" form of face-lift – Pyotr began to visit the opera regularly and to study as much music as he could. In the days before radio or recorded music, the only way of getting to know the orchestral repertoire was by playing it through in piano versions; and the music was often difficult to find.

In May 1859, aged just nineteen, Pyotr graduated from the School of Jurisprudence, intending to enter the Ministry of Justice. To ordinary Russians, civil servants were then people to be shunned and hated: they represented petty officialdom and oppression. Tchaikovsky was not naturally suited to such a job: he was not really interested in politics, and he was once said to have absentmindedly torn up an important document and chewed up the scraps while talking about something completely different. "As soon as I have any money, I just squander it on pleasure – it's a vulgar, silly weakness," he once wrote to his sister Alexandra. Convinced that his own artistic talent was negligible – "they've made an official of me, though a poor one" – he amused himself by visiting the opera and the ballet in the evenings, and playing the piano at dances and parties. In the summer of 1861 he and a friend set off on a European tour. Bored by Germany and Holland, depressed by the stuffy atmosphere of Victorian London (he always hated the British), Pyotr then discovered the delights of Second-Empire Paris. He immediately fell in love with the glittering, frivolous city where life was enjoyed to the full on the spacious boulevards, in elegant cafés, or in the theaters where the witty, satirical, and tuneful music of Offenbach was all the rage. On returning to Russia he made up his mind to become a musician, and diligently tackled the study of counterpoint and thoroughbass at classes held by the Russian Musical Society. Then, in September 1862, the famous pianist and composer Anton Rubinstein opened a new Conservatory in St. Petersburg. Tchaikovsky immediately enrolled as one of

1854-1866

the first students: "Whether I become a famous composer or just a struggling teacher, it's all the same . . . I'll have no right to complain any more." He worked hard, found small, cheap quarters, gave up going to smart parties, and grew his hair long – although he had not yet acquired his characteristically Russian bushy beard. Meanwhile, he resigned his job at the Ministry and scraped a poor living from teaching and accompanying. Although his future was far from secure, he was happier than before.

Tchaikovsky's relationship with Rubinstein, one of the most influential teachers and finest conductors of his time,

Tchaikovsky as a student

Anton (left) and Nikolay Rubinstein

was never an easy one. Rubinstein had received an old-fashioned German training in Berlin, and his arrogant intolerance made him many enemies. In particular, he bitterly resented anything new and original. The most important student piece that Tchaikovsky composed was an overture called *The Storm*, inspired by a play by the Russian dramatist Ostrovsky. It concerns a young married woman, who is humiliated and driven to suicide by her domineering mother-in-law. (The Czech composer Janáček later set the play as an opera.) Katya's persecution, within a straitlaced society that doesn't understand her, struck a sympathetic chord with Tchaikovsky, and instead of a dry, academic exercise, he turned in a colorful, dramatic piece of "program music," which used unusual instruments such as the harp, cor anglais (a low oboe), and tuba, and sounds genuinely "Russian." Rubinstein was furious: the piece was not at all the kind of thing he expected. And he was no more complimentary about Tchaikovsky's graduation exercise, a cantata setting Schiller's *Ode to Joy* (which Beethoven used in the Finale of his Ninth Symphony). The cantata was performed on January 12, 1866, in the presence of a distinguished audience – but not the composer, who was unable to face the pressure of the occasion. Although it attracted a lot of criticism, and Rubinstein threatened to withhold Tchaikovsky's diploma, no one could deny his outstanding talent, and two days later he graduated from the Conservatory. Just one person, the critic Hermann Laroche, consoled Tchaikovsky for his less-than-triumphant exit: "I think you possess the greatest talent in Russia today," he wrote perceptively. "I see you as the greatest, indeed the only, hope for our musical future . . . You may not produce anything of note for five years or so. But those mature works will surpass everything since Glinka."

3 In Search of Maturity

Unlike many penniless music students, both then and now, Tchaikovsky was fortunate in having a job waiting for him. The previous September, Anton Rubinstein's brother Nikolay had offered him employment as a harmony teacher in the Moscow branch of the Russian Musical Society – shortly to become the Moscow Conservatory, with Nikolay Rubinstein as its director. So Tchaikovsky moved to Moscow, the ancient Slav capital of Russia where, in complete contrast to the Western sophistication of St. Petersburg, the influence of the East abounded, in colorful onion-domed churches, clanging bells, and massive medieval fortresses.

A great Russian bear of a man, full of energy, and

1866-1870

The Moscow Conservatory

Moscow: the Kremlin

9

addicted to working hard, drinking hard, and gambling, Nikolay Rubinstein welcomed Tchaikovsky into his circle of friends, which included writers, musicians, and publishers. The sensitive composer found teaching rather a strain, but quickly discovered a taste for alcohol during the long evenings spent in Rubinstein's company. Tchaikovsky's first musical success came when Rubinstein conducted his Overture in F major at a concert on March 16, 1866, and he immediately began work on a symphony; but then he happened to read an extremely caustic review of his graduation cantata. Profoundly hurt, he had a minor breakdown; he was unable to sleep, suffered from terrible headaches, and was convinced that he was going to die. Normally he would have sought peace and security with his sister and her husband Lev Davidov at Kamenka, where he often spent the summers. But there had been an attempt on the Tsar's life, the roads were patrolled by secret police, and Tchaikovsky was unable to escape. Instead, he struggled on with his symphony, trying to cope with his nervous problems, which got worse every time he picked up his pen. Even so, he still managed to write a *Festival Overture* celebrating the wedding of the Tsarevich (the Tsar's son): for this he received a flashy pair of cuff-links, which he promptly sold.

Tchaikovsky would never find writing symphonies easy: to the end of his life he struggled to master both form and musical content. The Symphony No. 1, "Winter Daydreams," is modelled on Mendelssohn's "Italian" and "Scotch" symphonies – both musical paintings of landscapes – and although Tchaikovsky thought it had "glaring deficiencies," he always had a soft spot for it, calling it "a sweet sin of my youth." The first and second movements both have subtitles: "Daydreams of a Winter Journey" and "Land of Desolation, Land of Mists". Both use tunes influenced by Russian folk-melodies, and evoke the bleak Russian countryside in the grip of winter. The Symphony was first performed complete in February 1868 with Rubinstein conducting, and Tchaikovsky revised it a few years later.

Moscow: St. Basil's Cathedral

1800-1870

Theme from the slow movement of Symphony No.1 ("Winter Daydreams")

Désirée Artôt

With a symphony under his belt, Tchaikovsky then announced that he was going to start work on an opera, *The Voyevoda* (a Russian nobleman), to a libretto by Ostrovsky. Halfway through, he lost the libretto (a disaster in pre-photocopying days), and although poor Ostrovsky tried hard to reconstruct it, he eventually gave up in despair, leaving Tchaikovsky to write the text as well as the music. While he was working on the opera, he and his brother Anatoly spent a holiday at a spa on the Estonian coast with Vera and Elizaveta Davidova, sisters-in-law to their own sister. Pyotr knew them well, having spent time with them on holiday at Kamenka, and it seems that Vera was greatly attracted to the young composer. But although Tchaikovsky wrote a set of charming piano pieces for her, of which the last is the popular "Song without Words," he felt nothing for her beyond friendship. In fact, the only serious love interest that Tchaikovsky ever showed in a woman was for a young and talented Belgian soprano named Désirée Artôt, who visited Moscow with an Italian opera company in the autumn of 1868. Tchaikovsky wrote some music for her, and even began to discuss marriage plans with his family; but Désirée's formidable mother, scenting trouble, took matters in hand, and a few months later Tchaikovsky heard that his beloved had married a Spanish baritone in Warsaw. Although distressed by the news, Tchaikovsky quickly recovered from the disappointment.

A Russian peasant scene

"Song without Words" from "Souvenir de Hapsal"

Allegretto grazioso e cantabile

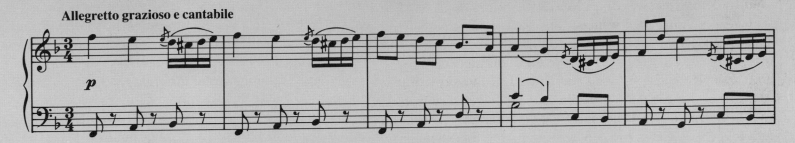

1866-1870

Mily Balakirev,
drawn by Bakst

Alexander Borodin,
painted by Repin

L BAKST

Nikolay Rimsky-Korsakov

Meanwhile, *The Voyevoda* had progressed quickly. In February 1868, Tchaikovsky was invited to conduct some dances from it at a charity concert. On the platform, he suffered an attack of blind panic, forgot the music, and gave all the wrong leads to the orchestra. Fortunately the players simply ignored him, and got through the pieces as best they could. Afterwards, Tchaikovsky confessed to a friend that he had been convinced his head would fall off while he was conducting, and he had held on to his beard throughout. Despite this fiasco, the music from *Voyevoda* was well received, even by the formidable group of St. Petersburg composers known as the "Mighty Handful," who dominated Russian composition at that time, and Tchaikovsky was promised a performance at the Bolshoy Theater in Moscow.

The Mighty Handful, also known as "The Five," was a curious crowd of dedicated drinkers, who were largely amateur composers. Borodin (composer of the famous "Polovtsian Dances") worked as a chemist; César Cui as a military engineer; while the most gifted, Modest Musorgsky (composer of the magnificent opera *Boris Godunov*), was a civil servant whom the rest regarded with a certain contempt. The most professional of the bunch, Nikolay Rimsky-Korsakov, was an accomplished and skillful orchestrator. His operas, mostly based on Russian folk-themes, were very popular in their time, while his attractive orchestral works such as *Sheherazade* and the famous *Spanish Capriccio* are still often heard today. But it was their self-appointed leader, Mily Balakirev, whose judgement everyone feared. A fierce nationalist, Balakirev actively detested any art that was not Russian. His aim was to establish truly national music, and much of the "Handful's" time was spent criticizing and rewriting other people's compositions – including each other's – in the "approved" style.

So when Tchaikovsky humbly sent the score of a new tone-poem, *Fate*, to Balakirev, asking him to accept its dedication, it should have come as no surprise that he received in return a long letter, listing the music's defects and suggesting major "improvements." Tchaikovsky revered Balakirev so much and wanted his recognition so badly, that he meekly accepted the criticism and tore the piece up.

On February 11, 1869, *The Voyevoda* was performed at the Bolshoy Theater in Moscow. At first it seemed to be a success, but it closed after only five performances. The critics were not impressed, and Tchaikovsky later cannibalized bits of it for other pieces. The same fate awaited his next stage work, the fairy opera *Undine*. Then, in the autumn of 1869, Tchaikovsky and Balakirev finally met in Moscow. Never

The Bolshoy Theater

happier than when dabbling in other people's work, Balakirev encouraged Tchaikovsky to begin a new tone-poem, based on Shakespeare's tragedy *Romeo and Juliet*. The subject-matter – young love crushed by the hostile forces of fate – fired Tchaikovsky's imagination. In his powerfully dramatic setting, those favorite Russian obsessions – love and death – are framed by vivid musical skirmishes between the rival families. Romeo and Juliet's devastating passion is represented by a powerful, soaring theme, which at the end collapses into a somber death-march, accompanied by funereal drum-rolls. After many revisions and modifications (suggested, naturally, by Balakirev), *Romeo and Juliet* was heard for the first time at a concert in Moscow in March 1870. Although the audience was slow to appreciate it, the score was quickly published, and it has since become one of Tchaikovsky's most popular works. Laroche's prophecy, made four years earlier, had come to pass.

Above: Modest Musorgsky, painted by Repin
Left: César Cui, drawn by Repin

15

Love theme from "Romeo and Juliet"

Tchaikovsky with two of his brothers and a friend (from right to left, Pyotr Ilyich Tchaikovsky, Anatoly Tchaikovsky, Nikolay Kondratyev, Ippolit Tchaikovsky)

4 The Nationalist

Although he was beginning to develop a genuine musical personality, Tchaikovsky's journey towards artistic maturity was painful. On the one hand, he had been trained in the cosmopolitan Western tradition, while on the other, he was as eager to discover his own Russian roots as any of the Mighty Handful. Though his songs are reminiscent of those turned out by German and French composers (one of the best is a setting of Goethe, known in English as "None but the lonely heart"), he diligently studied and arranged Russian folk songs, which he then used in his own music, such as the famous second movement (Andante cantabile) of his first string quartet. "As far as the Russian element in my music is concerned, i.e. the relationship between folk songs and my melodies and harmonies, this is because I grew up in the provinces, imbued from earliest childhood with the indescribable beauty of the characteristic features of Russian folk-music . . . because I am Russian in the truest sense of the word," he wrote, several years later. Meanwhile he continued to spend his holidays at Kamenka, where his adored sister Alexandra was bringing up her family in the peace and seclusion of the Russian countryside. Tchaikovsky, who loved his nieces and nephews, was deeply envious: "I long for the sound of children's voices and to share in little domestic matters — in short, for family life," he wrote to Alexandra from Moscow, where he felt lonely, bored and neglected.

1870-1875

Kamenka, home of Tchaikovsky's sister

He was not, however, short of friends, although his relationships with several young men were starting to cause disconcerting rumors and gossip in musical circles. Vladimir Shilovsky, a wealthy and talented young musician suffering from tuberculosis, fell seriously ill in Paris in 1870, and Tchaikovsky immediately rushed off to join him there. But the outbreak of the Franco-Prussian War drove them to Germany (where they found Nikolay Rubinstein – true to form – gambling away his last rubles at Wiesbaden), and then to Switzerland and Austria. The two spent further holidays together over the next two years, including a trip to the French Riviera – paid for by Shilovsky.

In the autumn of 1871 Tchaikovsky finally found a small apartment of his own in Moscow, furnished with a sofa, a few chairs and two pictures, one a portrait of Anton Rubinstein. He even took on a valet, and to pay for all this extravagance, he began to supplement his small income as a Conservatory professor by writing music criticism for the

A Russian peasant scene

Moscow Gazette. His state of mind, however, remained generally depressed. "I feel old, and unable to enjoy anything," he wrote – at the ripe old age of thirty-one – to his brother Anatoly. "I live on my memories and my hopes. But what is left to hope for?" The answer was work: in May 1872 he finished another opera, *The Oprichnik* (a bloodthirsty melodrama set in the reign of Ivan the Terrible), and, while staying at Kamenka during the summer, he began work on his Second Symphony. Known as the "Little Russian," it is one of Tchaikovsky's most nationalistic works, and uses several genuine Ukrainian folk-tunes. These presented a compositional problem: while composers such as Beethoven and Brahms were able to build up a powerful, integrated symphonic structure from short thematic motifs and rhythmic patterns, a folk-tune – though often an attractive melody – is less flexible. It is complete in itself, and Russian folk-melodies in particular tend to curl back on themselves in a repetitive, Oriental-sounding pattern. Composers such as Dvořák in Bohemia, Grieg in Norway, and (much later) Vaughan Williams in England encountered similar problems when using national folk-songs in their own pieces, and it is a tribute to Tchaikovsky's inventiveness

Peasants drinking tea

that he managed to devise so many imaginative ways of extending and weaving such tunes into the fabric of his orchestral works.

Encouraged by the enthusiastic reception given to the new symphony in February 1873 (one critic called it "one of the most important creations of the entire Russian school"), Tchaikovsky began work on some incidental music for a play by Ostrovsky called *The Snow Maiden*. (Rimsky-Korsakov later wrote an opera on the same subject.) After another holiday in Europe – alone, this time – he spent several blissful days on Shilovsky's estate near Kiev, where, in a spirit of serene exaltation, he wandered in the woods during the day, over the empty steppes in the evening, and sat at the open window by night, listening to the profound silence. In less than two weeks, he had sketched out a new

"symphonic fantasia" called *The Tempest*, based on Shakespeare's elusive, magical play. But although it offered plenty of scope for musical tone-painting (this time of the sea, the contrast between the free spirit Ariel and the monster Caliban, and the love between Ferdinand and Miranda), the subject failed to fire Tchaikovsky's imagination as *Romeo and Juliet* had done. Nevertheless, *The Tempest* was a great success at its first performance in Moscow in December.

On April 24, 1874, *The Oprichnik* was first performed at the Maryinsky Theater in St. Petersburg. Tchaikovsky was awarded a prize, and a celebratory supper was given in his honor by the Russian Musical Society; but yet again, the reviews were depressing – and the composer found himself agreeing with the critics. "*The Oprichnik* torments me," he confided. This insecurity led him to make a serious error of

1870-1875

The Maryinsky Theater, St. Petersburg

19

judgement. His next opera, *Vakula the Smith*, was written for entry in a competition organized by the Russian Musical Society. Tchaikovsky mistook the closing date for entries, and completed the piece a year ahead of time. In an unfortunate attempt to bolster his own self-confidence, he tried to exert pressure on the Musical Society and on individual judges, including Rimsky-Korsakov and Nikolay Rubinstein, to have his opera performed even before the competition had opened. Although his setting was by far the best, he was – not surprisingly – criticized for unprofessional behavior. Based on Gogol's delightful fantasy *Christmas Eve* (also the subject of a later opera by Rimsky-Korsakov), *Vakula* drew from Tchaikovsky some of his most characteristically Slavic music. Although it won first prize, the fickle public were unimpressed by it, and it was abandoned. Nine years later, it was heavily revised under the new title *The Slippers*.

Shortly afterwards his pride received another blow when, in November 1874, he began work on a piano concerto. No virtuoso pianist himself, he decided to turn to Nikolay Rubinstein for technical advice. At a private play-through at the Conservatory, Rubinstein listened to the first movement in complete silence. "Not a word, not a single remark!...I summoned up my patience and played

through to the end. Still silence. I got up and asked, 'Well?'" Then, said Tchaikovsky, "a torrent of abuse poured from Rubinstein's lips. The concerto was 'worthless, unplayable, clumsy, badly written, vulgar, plagiaristic, and needed to be thrown away and completely reworked.' Anyone would have thought I was a madman, a stupid, senseless hack who had come to lay his rubbish before a great musician." Deeply shocked, the composer left the room without a word. Rubinstein, seeing how hurt he was, followed him, and tried to soften the blow by saying that if Tchaikovsky would agree to revise the piece, he would do him the honor of playing it in public. "I shall not alter a single note," answered Tchaikovsky. "The work will be published exactly as it stands!"

Tchaikovsky's instinct was right. The First Piano Concerto – with the grand sweep of its opening gesture, its alternation of brilliant virtuosity with delicately scored melodies, its exhilarating contrasts of mood and tempo – has established itself as one of the most famous and popular piano concertos ever written. Tchaikovsky dedicated the piece to the German conductor and pianist Hans von Bülow, who gave its premiere in Boston on an American tour. Four years later Rubinstein apologized to Tchaikovsky and admitted his mistake.

20

Theme from Piano Concerto No.1 *(original key B flat minor)*

5 Crisis

Meanwhile, Tchaikovsky had emerged from the most "nationalistic" phase of his career. Over the summer of 1875, again spent with the Davidovs, he composed another symphony, this time in five movements, two of them in dance styles. The Finale, a cheerful "Tempo di polacca," later gave rise to the work's nickname, the "Polish" Symphony. (In fact, it has nothing to do with Poland at all.) In August Tchaikovsky also began work on the first of his famous sequence of ballets, *Swan Lake*, which he had been asked to write for the Imperial Theater in Moscow. The story is simple: Prince Siegfried is under pressure to choose a bride. He falls in love with a mysterious girl, who, with her attendants, has been turned into a swan by a magician. The spell can only be broken by a proposal of marriage. Siegfried swears undying love to her; but on the day of their engagement, he is fooled into promising marriage to her "double," the magician's daughter Odile. Odette, the real swan princess, dies of grief at Siegfried's betrayal, and the lovers sink beneath the waters of the Swan Lake. The first performance in March 1877 was spoilt by poor scenery, an orchestra unable to cope with such complicated music (including some fiendishly difficult violin solos), terrible choreography, and an incompetent conductor. But *Swan Lake* survived, and is now recognized as one of the greatest nineteenth-century ballets.

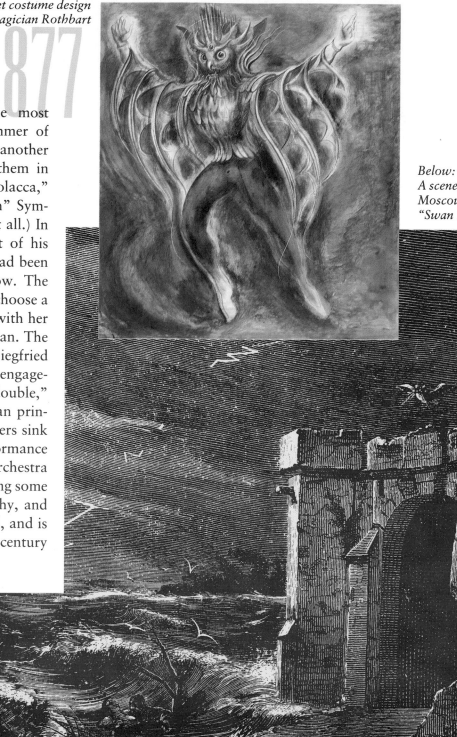

*Below:
A scene from the 1877
Moscow production of
"Swan Lake"*

"Dance of the Little Swans" from "Swan Lake"

The theater at Bayreuth

At the beginning of 1876, Tchaikovsky once more left Moscow for Paris, where he was completely bowled over by Bizet's masterpiece, *Carmen*. Both the music and the plot — once more a tale of ill-starred passion — appealed greatly, and he began to look for a similar subject. In fact, his own music had much in common with Bizet's, in its sensuous melodies, its ability to create an "atmosphere," and the skillful use of orchestral color. Tchaikovsky's own reputation as a composer was beginning to spread across Europe, and soon after returning to Moscow he was invited to attend the opening of the opera house at Bayreuth. Wagner's great "Ring" cycle, heard for the first time that year, both amazed and exhausted Tchaikovsky. "The *Ring of the Nibelung* is one of the most significant events in artistic history . . . one of the most gigantic artistic enterprises ever conceived by the human mind," he wrote. That autumn his experiences bore fruit in a new work. "I've just finished the composition of a new work, the symphonic fantasia *Francesca da Rimini*. I've worked on it *con amore*, and believe it will be a success," he

wrote to his brother. His fellow-composers agreed with him, but despite a vivid depiction of the gates of Hell (with its famous inscription "Abandon hope, all ye that enter here"), the whirlwind that tosses the lovers Paolo and Francesca around for all eternity, and the wistful central love-theme, Tchaikovsky's response to Dante's moving account of tragic passion has never achieved the popularity of *Romeo and Juliet*. Perhaps his own overwrought mood at the time had something to do with it: in complete contrast to his tormented obsession with love and death, the delicate poise of the "Rococo" variations for cello and orchestra (written for a cellist friend) shows the composer taking refuge in the order and grace of a bygone world.

Richard Wagner

Theme from "Rococo Variations"

In August 1876, Modest Tchaikovsky was horrified to receive a letter from his brother: "I am now at a critical point in my life. I shall tell you about it in more detail soon, but in the meantime, you should know that I have decided to get married. This is irrevocable." Tchaikovsky had finally been forced to confront his true nature, something from which he had spent thirty-six years trying desperately to escape: the unavoidable fact that he was homosexual.

In the later nineteenth century, homosexuality was only admitted in private: it was certainly not socially acceptable, and would remain illegal for almost another century. Only two decades later, in 1895, English society was rocked to the core by the notorious trial of the brilliant wit and playwright, Oscar Wilde, for homosexual "offences." Despite enjoying the patronage of royalty, Wilde was condemned to the ultimate disgrace of two years' hard labor, which ruined his health, as well as his reputation. Such were the dangers of publicly "coming out" – or at least, of getting caught.

Tchaikovsky himself regarded his sexuality as a vice, as an unbearable shame to be hidden and bitterly regretted: or even as his "fate," which had to be fought and overcome. He had certainly had several affairs with men, but what he wanted was "normality" – marriage and children; and he was determined to find himself a wife: "the beautiful, still-undiscovered being who will make me change my way of life." Unfortunately the realities of achieving this impossible dream escaped him: one of his friends remarked that what Tchaikovsky really needed was a widow or spinster who would understand him, but in a sexless relationship.

As Fate would have it, such a person was shortly to enter his life. Nadezhda von Meck, then in her mid-forties, was the widow of an engineer. She had married him at sixteen, had twelve children, and through her enormous energy and business sense, had transformed him from a poor government official into a highly successful and enormously wealthy railway tycoon. In 1876 her husband found out that his youngest daughter was not his, but the child of his secretary, with whom Nadezhda had been having an affair. The shock of this revelation caused a fatal heart attack, which left his guilty widow a multimillionairess.

After her husband's sudden death, Nadezhda began to use some of her wealth as a patroness of the arts. She had heard and enjoyed some of Tchaikovsky's music, and when she found out that he had financial problems, she began to commission pieces from him, and then to give him presents of money. The one condition she imposed was that they

Nadezhda von Meck

1875-1877

The von Meck family. Karl von Meck is sitting at the back: his secretary, Mme von Meck's lover, is in front

Despite the fears of his family and friends, the marriage went ahead on July 18, 1877. That evening, the couple took the train to St. Petersburg to visit Tchaikovsky's father, and the composer's nightmare began. "I was almost screaming, choked up with sobs," he wrote to his brother. Despite Tchaikovsky's attempts to explain to his fiancée that any physical contact between them would be impossible, Antonina had either not understood, or naïvely believed – as have many other women in her situation – that she could "reform" her husband. Aged twenty-eight, she was by no

should never meet: although their strange relationship (carried on through over 1100 letters) was to last nearly fourteen years, they only met twice, by accident, and hurried past without greeting each other.

However, Tchaikovsky's domestic longings were still not satisfied. In the spring of 1877, while working on his new symphony, he received a series of letters from a student named Antonina Milyukova, declaring that she loved him. Against his better judgement, Tchaikovsky met the persistent girl, and told her that he could not return her love. At that moment, ironically, his attention was drawn to Pushkin's play *Eugene Onegin* as a potential opera-subject. In the play's central scene, the young and innocent heroine writes a letter to her hero, Eugene Onegin, declaring her love for him. The worldly-wise Onegin scornfully rejects Tatyana's timid advances, causing her shame and distress. Tchaikovsky was immediately struck by the coincidence in his own life, and rashly proposed marriage to Antonina without further thought.

Tchaikovsky and his bride, Antonina

means the raving nymphomaniac of Ken Russell's notorious film *The Music Lovers*, but she was not very bright, and inclined to be mentally unstable – she apparently believed that all men fell in love with her at first sight.

Just over a week later, Tchaikovsky was in utter despair. In a letter to Madame von Meck he explained that he had felt duty-bound to marry Antonina, having thoughtlessly encouraged her in the first place, but that he had soon realized that his wife was "abhorrent" to him – through no fault of her own. "Death seemed to me the only way out – but suicide was unthinkable," he wrote. His patroness, who almost certainly knew of his homosexuality, responded with a generous loan which allowed Tchaikovsky to flee Moscow and his wife, going first to his sister at Kamenka, and then on to Madame von Meck's country estate at Brailov in the Caucasus. But by September he knew he must return to Moscow. For a miserable fortnight, he and Antonina tried to resume married life, until he could bear the strain no longer: one freezing night he waded out into the icy river and stood there until he was sure he would catch pneumonia and die. But he survived unscathed, and so on October 6 he fled once again, this time to his brother Anatoly in St. Petersburg. Anatoly put him straight to bed, where he lay in a coma for two days. He was then told by a specialist that he should never try to see his wife again. His family and friends broke the news to Antonina, who at first received it calmly; but when the question of divorce arose, she refused to consent to it. From then on, her own mental condition disintegrated: she produced a series of illegitimate children (which gave Tchaikovsky grounds for divorce), and was finally certified as insane and placed in an asylum in 1896. She outlived her husband by twenty-four years, convinced to the end that he was still madly in love with her.

28

A letter from Tchaikovsky to Mme von Meck, written around the time of his marriage

6 Recovery

When Madame von Meck learned what had happened, she immediately arranged for Tchaikovsky to receive a regular allowance of 6000 rubles. Meanwhile, the composer and his brother Anatoly had set out on a European tour through Paris, Florence, Rome, Venice, and Vienna, hoping to put the whole disastrous business firmly behind them. By January 1878 Tchaikovsky had finished his Fourth Symphony, the first of his mature symphonic works. It combines his love of the Russian people, the countryside, folk-music and dancing – all overshadowed by his ever-present sense of fate. He dedicated it "to my best friend" (Madame von Meck). "I am sure that as far as style and form are concerned, it represents a forward step in my development," he wrote to her. "There is a program to our symphony ... the introduction is the seed of the whole work ... this is Fate, the fatal force which prevents the realization of our hopes of happiness ... It is inescapable, and can never be avoided ... O joy! at last a sweet and tender vision appears. Some bright, charming human form passes, beckoning. How lovely! ... All that was gloomy, despairing, is forgotten.

Happiness is here! No! These were dreams, and Fate awakens us harshly. Thus, life perpetually alternates between grim reality and fleeting dreams of happiness ..."

In those words Tchaikovsky made it clear that outward circumstances did affect his inner, creative life, though he stressed that "the artist lives a double life, one everyday, human, the other artistic; and these two lives sometimes do not coincide." The other three movements of the symphony, according to Tchaikovsky, represented "another phase of depression," a kind of wistful longing for the past; the third movement – the famous Scherzo in which the string players pluck throughout – "consists of elusive thoughts of the kind that flit through the mind when one is a little drunk ... a rowdy peasant, a street song, a distant military parade ..." And in the last, a scene of innocent merry-making is interrupted once again by the powerful "Fate" theme.

Peasants haymaking

1878

Theme from the slow movement of Symphony No.4

The other major work which occupied him during the period of his ill-fated marriage was the opera *Eugene Onegin* which, in a way, had brought it all about. Alexander Pushkin, who died in a duel at thirty-eight, was one of Russia's greatest poets, a heroic character who was always getting into trouble with the political censors. He was a kind of Russian Goethe, whose work reflected a vast range of human experience, but who was never accepted by narrow-minded officialdom. *Eugene Onegin*, his novel in verse, concerns two sisters, the lively Olga and the shy, gentle Tatyana. Olga's fiancé, Lensky, brings his friend Eugene Onegin home, and Tatyana falls in love with him. But the cynical Onegin rejects her, and then enrages his friend Lensky by flirting with Olga at Tatyana's birthday dance. Lensky challenges Onegin to a duel, and is killed. Several years later, Onegin meets Tatyana again at a ball in St. Petersburg. She is now married to an elderly prince, who dotes on her. Onegin realizes his terrible mistake. He declares his love for her, but Tatyana, although she still loves Onegin, chooses to stay faithful to her husband.

Alexander Pushkin

1878

Like the Fourth Symphony, *Eugene Onegin* offered opportunities for all Tchaikovsky's favorite themes: from exuberant dances to vivid scenes of Russian country life; from wild emotional outpourings such as the famous "Letter Scene" to songs of touching simplicity, such as Prince Gremin's aria in praise of his charming, innocent wife. But at first the opera made little impression, and it took several years to achieve the public success it deserved.

Theme from the Letter Scene of "Eugene Onegin"

31

CODA

*Maria Klimentova, the original Tatyana,
in the Letter Scene from "Eugene Onegin"*

1878

Yet another masterpiece emerged from this period of self-exile: the Violin Concerto, written in Switzerland and dedicated to the great Russian violinist and teacher Leopold Auer. At first, however, the concerto suffered the same fate as the First Piano Concerto: Auer claimed it was far too difficult and refused to play it. In 1881 another violinist, Adolf Brodsky, gave the first performance in Vienna, at which a famous critic declared that the music "gave off a bad smell." Just like the Piano Concerto, the Violin Concerto, with its powerfully lyrical opening theme, its nostalgic Canzonetta, and its exhilarating Finale in the style of a wild Cossack dance, is now established as one of the best-loved violin concertos, for players and audiences alike.

7 Return of the Wanderer

Tchaikovsky returned in April 1878 to a Russia torn by student riots, violence, terrorism, and outbreaks of infectious disease. Depressed by the prospect of teaching, and short of inspiration, he also had to try to persuade Antonina to agree to a divorce, though he was terrified that she might reveal the true reason for their separation. Nevertheless, he finished some smaller piano pieces, including the well-known "Chanson triste" (Sad Song) and the popular *Children's Album*. On returning to Moscow after his usual summer visits to Kamenka and Brailov, he took a decisive step: he resigned his teaching job at the Conservatory, and shortly afterwards set off on his travels once more. He was to spend the next few years constantly on the move, avoiding Moscow and St. Petersburg as much as possible. First he went to Florence, then to Paris, and to Clarens in Switzerland, where he worked on another opera about Joan of Arc. It was not one of his greatest successes. Back in Russia in the autumn he began a Second Piano Concerto, which has never been as popular as the First; while a further visit to Rome prompted the noisy, rather vulgar *Italian Capriccio*.

Tchaikovsky then returned to Russia, where he spent much of 1880 in the country. There he completed the Serenade for strings, and the piece most often associated with his name – the *1812 Overture*, a commemoration of the historic Russian defeat of Napoleon's army, written at Nikolay Rubinstein's request and now often played at popular concerts, complete with cannon effects. Tchaikovsky did not think much of it: "The Overture will be very loud and noisy . . . and probably artistically worthless. But the Serenade . . . is a piece from the heart . . ."

Florence

"Emperor's Hymn" from the "1812 Overture"

Left: Napoleon's retreat from Moscow, 1812

In Rome early in 1881, Tchaikovsky heard that his old patron, friend, drinking companion, father-figure and harsh critic Nikolay Rubinstein was mortally ill in Paris. By the time he arrived, hoping to say goodbye, Rubinstein had consumed his last dozen oysters and died happy. Tchaikovsky watched the coffin being loaded into a luggage van for the long train journey back to Russia; and in December he began work on a musical memorial. The Piano Trio, dedicated "to the memory of a great artist," was first played in private by Madame von Meck's own trio (whose pianist at that time was the young French student Claude Debussy). The second movement is a long set of variations, each based on an incident in Rubinstein's colorful life.

By now Tchaikovsky's music was being performed more often, though rarely with total success. Although his operas *Eugene Onegin* and *The Maid of Orleans* were quickly dropped, once the novelty of the premieres had worn off, he began work on another – a dark tale of Cossack intrigue, torture, and murder called *Mazeppa*, which nevertheless offered scope for fiery national dances, effective battle music, and touching love-scenes. *Mazeppa* was performed both in Moscow and St. Petersburg in February 1884, but Tchaikovsky left for Europe without attending the St. Petersburg premiere, much to the surprise of the new Tsar, Alexander III, who had commissioned three pieces from Tchaikovsky for his coronation. Nonetheless, in March, Tchaikovsky was summoned back to Russia to receive an official decoration – the Order of St. Vladimir (4th Class).

Tsar Alexander III

35

Tchaikovsky in later life

By now he was feeling the need to stop his restless wandering and settle down. Although he had turned down the Directorship of the Moscow Conservatory, his acceptance into the "establishment" was sealed when he was elected head of the Moscow branch of the Russian Musical Society. He also tried to find himself a permanent home. "I don't need land, just a cottage with a pretty garden . . . a stream would be nice, and if it were near a forest, so much the better," he wrote to Madame von Meck. Such a cottage was found at a place called Maidanovo, near Klin, in the countryside outside Moscow. Tchaikovsky settled down to a regular routine: reading, walking in the forest, working in the mornings and afternoons, playing cards or duets with friends in the evenings. "I am contented, happy, at peace,"

he wrote. And he renewed his acquaintance with Balakirev, broken off in irritation many years before. Balakirev had not changed at all: still unable to stop handing out advice, he persuaded Tchaikovsky to start work on a new symphony, based on Byron's heroic poem *Manfred*. Finished in October 1885, the *Manfred* Symphony — a brilliant and effective piece of program music which is not one of Tchaikovsky's numbered symphonies — owes a great deal to Berlioz's example, especially the *Symphonie fantastique* and *Harold in Italy*.

Once *Manfred* was finished, Tchaikovsky started yet another opera. *The Sorceress* is a story about an innkeeper's daughter who is courted by two princes — a father and son — with predictably disastrous consequences. The ridiculous plot left audiences cold. Tchaikovsky, by now accustomed to success, was deeply wounded by its failure. But he overcame his terror of conducting to direct both the first performances at the Maryinsky Theater in St. Petersburg in 1887, together with a concert of his own works which included the premiere of his fourth orchestral suite, a set of four Mozart arrangements. In December, he set out on his

Tchaikovsky's house and garden at Klin

Tchaikovsky's desk at Klin

first European concert tour as a conductor, meeting several famous composers: Brahms (whose music he disliked), Grieg, Busoni, Dvořák, and the eccentric Englishwoman Ethel Smyth. His tour was a triumphant success, particularly in Paris, where the current fashion was for all things Eastern and Slavonic. Even chilly, fog-bound London warmed to the music, if not to the man.

Exhausted by success, Tchaikovsky returned home in April 1888, and moved into a picturesque new house at Frolovskoye, near Klin, with an enchanting view and a beautiful garden. There he began a new symphony – the Fifth – whose famous opening theme represents "complete resignation before Fate." Unlike Beethoven, whose own Fifth Symphony is said to embody a heroic struggle against Fate, Tchaikovsky seemed to have come to terms with his personal tragedy, and accepted the "predestination of Providence" – although "murmurs, doubts, complaints" remain in the background. The famous horn solo at the start of the second movement ushers in some of the most radiant love-music ever written. The third movement is a seductive waltz, while the Finale returns to the "Providence" theme, now transformed and worked through to a triumphant ending. The Fifth Symphony has always been one of Tchaikovsky's most enduringly popular works, but shortly after its premiere, he realized that it had a hollow ring. "There is something repulsive about it, an excessive cheapness and insincerity, even artificiality," he wrote to Madame von Meck. It was as if he had a premonition of the real fate which awaited him – tragedy, not triumph.

37

Theme from the slow movement of Symphony No.5

8 Last Years

The Fifth Symphony was first performed under Tchaikovsky's baton in St. Petersburg on November 17, 1888. A week later he conducted the premiere of a new Shakespearian "fantasy overture," this time based on *Hamlet*. Though he loved Shakespeare, Tchaikovsky found it a "devilishly difficult" play, and unlike *Romeo and Juliet*, his version of *Hamlet* has no clearly defined program: it is more an atmospheric tone-poem, dominated by the brooding menace of Elsinore.

In December, he set to work on a new ballet score, based on the old French fairy tale of the beautiful Princess Aurora who is cursed by a wicked fairy at her christening, put to sleep on her seventeenth birthday for a hundred years, and finally woken by the kiss of a Prince. Whereas *Swan Lake* had been spoilt by poor staging, Tchaikovsky was now lucky to work with the great French ballet-master Marius Petipa, director of the Russian imperial ballet at the Bolshoy Theater. Petipa mapped out a detailed sequence of dances which greatly helped the composer, and he worked with real enthusiasm until forced to lay the work aside to go on another international concert tour. Once back home, he rushed to finish the score – "I work and I work and I work," he wrote – and in August, he was able to say that a "huge mountain" had fallen from his shoulders. *The Sleeping Beauty* certainly inspired some of Tchaikovsky's finest music: eloquent solo dances and tender duets; brilliant waltzes and colorful "divertissements," all neatly woven together by a strong and satisfying plot. Stravinsky, who owed a great deal to Tchaikovsky, later called it "the most convincing example of Tchaikovsky's great creative power," and it remains one of the greatest of all classical ballets.

A scene from "The Sleeping Beauty"

1888-1893

Waltz from "The Sleeping Beauty"

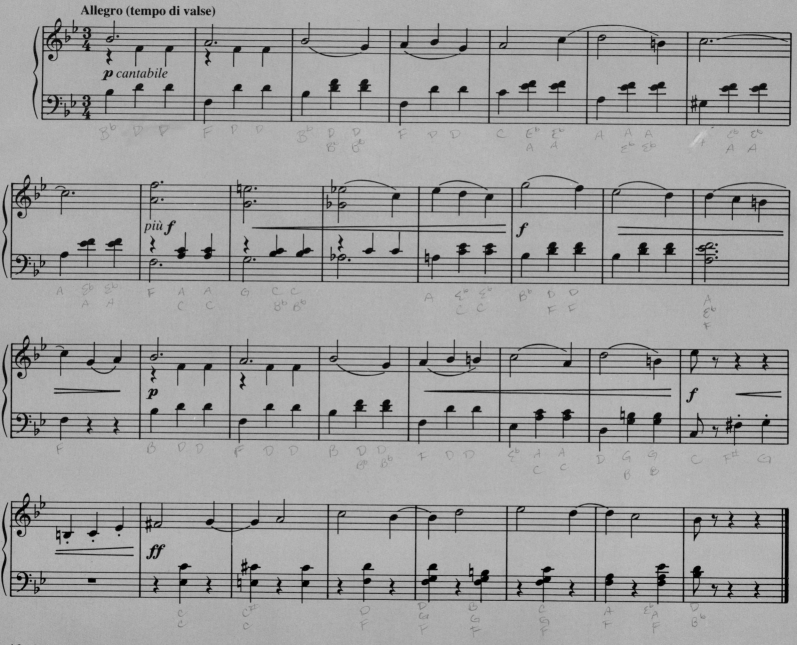

An early production of "The Queen of Spades," Act I

Shortly after the first performance of *The Sleeping Beauty*, in January 1890, Tchaikovsky once more left Russia, this time for Florence. There he began work on a new opera, *The Queen of Spades*. Pushkin's chilling supernatural tale of death and destruction caused by a young officer's obsession with gambling appealed to Tchaikovsky's gift for creating atmosphere, and he became deeply involved with his characters – he cried when writing the scene of Hermann's madness and suicide. To amuse himself once it was finished, he threw off a charming little diversion for six string instruments, called *Souvenir de Florence*.

Then, in early October, an unexpected bombshell threw him into utter despair. Madame von Meck informed him that she was in great financial trouble, and would therefore be ending both his allowance and their correspondence. By now, Tchaikovsky had no need of further money from her, and his immediate concern was for her own welfare. But he later found out that she had lied: she was not bankrupt, but merely wanted to break off their relationship. In fact, she was seriously ill with tuberculosis, her children were causing trouble, and her mental state was highly unbalanced. But Tchaikovsky knew none of this: he felt that his mother-figure had rejected him, which opened all the old wounds.

His one consolation was the instant success of *The*

41

third and last ballet; but in the meantime he accepted an invitation to conduct his own works in America. While in Paris, waiting to leave for America, he was horrified to read in a Russian newspaper of his beloved sister Alexandra's death, which his brother had tried to keep from him. Nevertheless, the tour went ahead, and though utterly miserable, Tchaikovsky was greatly impressed and heartened by the warmth and hospitality of his American hosts, and by the enthusiastic reception given to his music: his Piano Concerto was among the pieces played in a series of concerts which opened the new Carnegie Hall in New York. He also visited Baltimore, Philadelphia, and Niagara Falls, where he was alarmed to find himself taken on foot behind the massive curtain of water.

Back at home, Tchaikovsky returned to E. T. A. Hoffmann's fantasy story about a magic nutcracker which turns into a Prince, defeats the evil Mouse-King, and whisks Clara off into an enchanted kingdom of toys and sweets. Having earlier lamented that it would be impossible to depict the Sugar-Plum Fairy in music, he decided to use a new instrument which he had heard in Paris – the celeste. Its distinctive silvery sound has become one of *The Nut-*

Queen of Spades. This led to two more commissions from the Imperial Theater, for an opera and a ballet. In February 1891 Tchaikovsky started work on *The Nutcracker*, his

A vignette based on a scene from "The Nutcracker"

A stage set for Act II of "The Nutcracker," based on designs by Alexandre Benois

cracker's most memorable features, along with a delightful series of character dances for sugar-sticks, reed-pipes, Chinese tea, and two famous waltzes. But Tchaikovsky thought that the new ballet was "far weaker than *The Sleeping Beauty*," and all its best music is certainly packed into the much-performed orchestral suite.

Though this innocent child's paradise provided a temporary refuge from reality, Tchaikovsky's old enemy, Fate, was slowly catching up with him. Though still only fifty, he complained to his favorite nephew, Bob Davidov, that he was "getting worn out, [his] hair going white, [his] teeth falling out, [his] eyes getting worse." Even more depressing was the sense that his creative powers were failing – a morbid fear not helped by the lukewarm reception given in St. Petersburg just before Christmas 1892 to *The Nutcracker* and a new one-act opera, *Iolanta*, the story of a blind princess, set in medieval Provence.

At the end of December he left for his last European trip, visiting his old governess, Fanny Dürbach, in Switzerland. "She doesn't look her seventy years, and on the whole hasn't changed much at all," he wrote. "The past rose up so vividly before me that I seemed to breathe the air of

Votkinsk and hear my mother's voice distinctly . . ." After visiting Paris and Brussels he returned home to plan a new symphony. The previous year, he had sketched out an idea for a "Program Symphony," whose "ultimate essence is LIFE. First movement – all impulsive passion, confidence, feverish activity. Must be short. (Finale DEATH – result of collapse.) Second movement love; third disappointments;

Tchaikovsky in his Cambridge University doctoral robes

Tchaikovsky and his favorite nephew, Bob Davidov

fourth ends dying away (also short)." To his nephew Bob, Tchaikovsky wrote that the program of the new symphony "will remain a mystery to all . . . There will be much that is new, and incidentally the Finale won't be a loud Allegro, but on the contrary, a very slow-moving Adagio. You can't imagine what joy I feel in the conviction that my time is not yet over and that it is still possible to work . . ."

Tchaikovsky interrupted the new symphony to finish a set of six songs, and to collect an honorary doctorate from Cambridge University. He finished the symphony in August, and there is no doubt that it represents his musical farewell, a recognition that there was no further escape from the "Fate" that had always dogged him. After a huge, tightly constructed opening movement, which covers a vast emotional range from violent passion to a tender, yearning love theme, comes a waltz, whose five beats in the bar give it an odd limp, as if the couples had two of their legs tied together. The march which follows is brash and brilliant, but rather hollow; while the last movement, "Adagio Lamentoso," slides painfully downwards until it disintegrates into an anguished silence. There is no doubt that Tchaikovsky was foreseeing his own death.

Theme from Symphony No.6 ("Pathétique")

The apartment in Moscow where Tchaikovsky died

The new symphony was first performed in St. Petersburg on October 28, and Modest Tchaikovsky gave it the title "Pathétique," by which it has been known ever since. Just over a week later, Tchaikovsky was dead. For many years it was believed that he died of cholera, like his mother, from drinking unboiled water. But recently, evidence has come to light which suggests that he committed suicide. He was apparently having an affair with a young Russian aristocrat, whose uncle had written a letter to the Tsar, exposing the composer. The letter had been passed to a senior civil servant, who had attended the same school as Tchaikovsky. Fearing a public scandal, and disgrace to the "school uniform," he had summoned an emergency "court," consisting of several of Tchaikovsky's old schoolfellows. Tchaikovsky was asked to appear before the "court" on October 31, and after several hours' debate, he was ordered to kill himself. Within two days, he was fatally ill, probably from taking arsenic. "Leave me," he said to the doctors. "You can do nothing. I shall not recover." He was given the last rites, and at three o'clock in the morning of November 6, attended to the end by two of his brothers, his nephew, his faithful valet, and three doctors, he finally surrendered to Fate, which had pursued him so relentlessly.

1888-1893

Glossary of Musical Terms

Symphony A large-scale orchestral piece, usually in four separate movements (Tchaikovsky's Symphony No. 3 has five). The first and last are usually quick; the second slow and the third a scherzo (a fast piece, meaning literally "joke"). Tchaikovsky's Symphony No. 6 has a waltz for its second movement, a march for its third, and the last is very slow.

Overture A piece used normally to introduce an opera or other stage work, but in Tchaikovsky's day it was common to write separate overtures for performance as individual pieces, such as the "fantasy-overture" *Romeo and Juliet*, or the *1812 Overture*.

Symphonic Poem (or ballad, or fantasy) An orchestral piece in a single movement, usually describing in music a landscape, or a painting, or a scene from a book or play, or a person.

Serenade A light piece of orchestral or chamber music, designed to entertain.

Concerto A piece, often in three movements, for a solo instrument (most often piano, violin, or cello) and orchestra.

Sonata A piece in several movements for one or two instruments (such as piano alone, or violin and piano).

Chamber Music Pieces for a small but varied group of instruments, each playing an individual part.

Sextet A piece of chamber music for six instruments.

Quartet A piece of chamber music for four instruments. A string quartet consists of two violins, viola, and cello.

Trio A piece of chamber music for three instruments. A piano trio consists of piano, violin and cello.

Opera A drama set to music, usually in several acts.

Ballet A drama set to music, for dancers, rather than singers.

Incidental Music Music written to accompany a stage play.

Cantata A short piece of vocal music for one or more voices with instrumental accompaniment.

List of Works

Stage Works

12 operas, including *The Oprichnik* (1872); *Vakula the Smith* (1874, later revised as *The Slippers*, 1885); *Eugene Onegin* (1877–8); *The Maid of Orleans* (1878–9); *Mazeppa* (1881–3); *The Queen of Spades* (1890); *Iolanta* (1891). Incidental music for *The Snow Maiden* (1873); *Hamlet* (1891). 3 ballets: *Swan Lake* (1875–6); *The Sleeping Beauty* (1888–9); *The Nutcracker* (1891–2).

Vocal Music

About 20 cantatas and choruses; 12 pieces of miscellaneous sacred music; over 100 solo songs; 6 duets.

Orchestral Music

6 numbered symphonies: No. 1 in G minor ("Winter Daydreams," 1866); No. 2 in C minor ("Little Russian," 1872); No. 3 in D ("Polish," 1875); No. 4 in F minor (1877–8); No. 5 in E minor (1888); No. 6 in B minor ("Pathétique," 1893); *Manfred* Symphony in B minor (1885); sketches for Symphony No. 7 in E flat (unfinished). 7 overtures, including *The Storm* (1864); *Romeo and Juliet* (1869–70); *1812 Overture* (1880); *Hamlet* (1888). 4 symphonic poems: *Fate* (1868); *The Tempest* (1873); *Francesca da Rimini* (1876); *The Voyevoda* (1890–1).
4 orchestral suites: in D (1878–9); C (1883); G (1884); G ("Mozartiana," 1887). Slavonic March in B flat (1876); Festival Coronation March in D (1883); Italian Capriccio (1880); Serenade in C for strings (1880).
3 piano concertos: No. 1 in B flat minor (1874–5); No. 2 in G (1879–80); No. 3 (one movement only) in E flat (1893); Violin Concerto in D (1878); *Serenade mélancolique* for violin and orchestra (1875); "Rococo" Variations for cello and orchestra (1876); *Pezzo capriccioso* for cello and orchestra (1887).

Chamber music

3 completed string quartets, in D (1871); F (1874); E flat minor (1876); Piano Trio in A minor (1881–2); *Souvenir de Florence* for string sextet (1890); other short pieces.

Piano Music

About 112 piano pieces, including 2 sonatas; *Children's Album* (24 easy pieces); 12 Pieces of Moderate Difficulty; 6 pieces, Op. 51; 18 pieces, Op. 72.

Index

Picture Credits

The author and publishers have made every effort to identify the owners of the pictures used in this publication; they apologize for any inaccuracies and would like to thank the following:
(a, b and c indicate left to right/top to bottom)

Novosti Press Agency 4a, 4b, 4c, 8b, 9b, 17a, 17b, 26, 28, 36a, 37a, 37b, 44a, 44b.
John Massey Stewart 2, 3a, 5a, 5b, 7, 9a, 10a, 12a, 14a, 14c, 15c, 18a, 18b, 29, 31, 33, 35.
Mary Evans Picture Library 3b, 6a, 14b, 15a, 34, 36b.
ET Archive 19, 42 (Imperial Russian Theater), 22a (Royal Ballet Benevolent Fund), 22b (Bibliothèque de l'Opéra, Paris), 42a (Royal Ballet Benevolent Fund), 42b, 43 (London Festival Ballet).
Covent Garden Theater Museum 39, 41.
Elaine Gould (photos) 6b, 46.
Bibliothèque Nationale, Paris 12b.
Russian Museum, Leningrad 15b.
Publisher's collection frontispiece, 24a, 24b.

The cover shows a portrait of Tchaikovsky (Mary Evans Picture Library) against a 19th-century view of St. Petersburg (John Massey Stewart).

The author wishes to acknowledge her debt to many sources, including John Warrack: *Tchaikovsky* (London, 1973); and David Brown: *Tchaikovsky: A Biographical and Critical Study* (London, 1978–1991). She also wishes to thank Richard King, editor of the *Composer's World* series, for his invaluable help with the text and with picture research.